Praise for LITANY OF FLIGHTS

Winner of the Paraclete Poetry Prize

"*Litany of Flights* turns its gaze to the natural world and to the heightened sacramental reality with which, as Hopkins puts it, all the created order is *charged*. At every turn, these mysteries are grounded in the sensory details of the world we apprehend, tree, sun, and star, squirrel and deer, fruit and flower, hawk and dove."
—Sally Thomas, author of *Motherland*

"Hogan's collection is lush with rivers, moonlight, and flowers. It is also sharp with scrub brush, lightning, and flame. Like the Scripture she draws from, her poems both comfort and unsettle with fierce imagery: 'You wait for me to discover your love among the leaves and thorns . . . I join / your written roses in swaying dance, in blood-red bloom of belonging.' Her poems are an invitation directly into the heart of this swaying dance. This is a debut that will draw you into wonder without letting go."
—Tania Runyan, author of *What Will Soon Take Place*

"Laura Reece Hogan combines the rich language of Gerard Manley Hopkins with the fierce passion of Elizabeth Barrett Browning to become a twenty-first-century singer of the ancient Song of Songs. A new, loving, musical voice that you will want to hear and incorporate into your prayers."
—Paul J. Willis, author of *Deer at Twilight: Poems from the North Cascades*

"Some poets say their poems are borne in them; some believe poems come *through*: that the writer is merely the vessel. Such poets often take less credit for that voice of which they are the vehicle. These are the poets who give thanks and who praise. They come straight out of the mystical tradition, locked in a dance with the music and lyricism of St. Francis, Hopkins, St. John of the Cross, Herbert, Rumi, and Kabir. Laura Reece Hogan adds her name to this tradition in *Litany of Flights*.
She is a true poet, and this is a sensational debut."
—**David Keplinger,** author of *The Long Answer: New and Selected Poems*

"Hogan never yearns to escape this world, or the hurt and pain of living in it—rather her poems yearn to enter the world ever more deeply. What links them is their posture of prayer: the work of paring away what is nonessential in the speaker until, hollowed, like the bones of birds, she is light enough for flight."
—**Robert Cording,** author of *Walking with Ruskin*, and Professor Emeritus at College of the Holy Cross

"It is a rare privilege these days to dive into a poetry collection and find that the word that keeps reverberating in your ear is joy: from 'vats of joy' to 'cascades of joy,' from 'living in joy' to 'the joy in spilling praise.' Yet, joy does not come easy in *Litany of Flights*, for there are 'clefts of night' and 'barren months,' a church that burns, its cross 'tumbling into the nave like a sparkler.' Elsewhere, longing is a 'grounded bird' that 'thrashes against metal.' But the longing that animates this exquisite collection is for the One Who never fails, Who comes in cloud and burning bush, Who consumes and fulfills. And Laura Hogan knows this, viscerally. No wonder her poetry brims with joy; she knows what it is to be a creature in love with her Creator, thus able to offer—credibly—joy as the 'full flower of love.'"
—**Sofia Starnes,** former Virginia Poet Laureate, author of *The Consequence of Moonlight*

POEMS

LITANY OF FLIGHTS

LAURA REECE HOGAN

PARACLETE PRESS
BREWSTER, MASSACHUSETTS

2020

First
Printing

Litany of Flights: Poems

Copyright © 2020 by
Laura Reece Hogan

ISBN 978-1-64060-610-4

The excerpt from Rainer Maria Rilke
on page ix is from "Going Blind," *The
Selected Poetry of Rainer Maria Rilke*, ed. and
trans. by Stephen Mitchell
(New York: Vintage,
1989), 33.

The Paraclete Press name and logo (dove on cross)
are trademarks of Paraclete Press, Inc.

Library of Congress Cataloging-in-Publication Data
Names: Hogan, Laura Reece, 1966- author.
Title: Litany of flights : poems / Laura Reece
Hogan.
Description: Brewster, Massachusetts : Paraclete
Press, 2020. | Summary:
"Litany of Flights is a luminous examination of the
journey of the soul,
from moments of loss to moments of incandescent transformation"--
Provided by publisher.
Identifiers: LCCN 2020024411 (print) | LCCN 2020024412 (ebook) | ISBN
9781640606104 | ISBN 9781640606111 (epub) | ISBN 9781640606128 (pdf)
Subjects: LCGFT: Poetry.
Classification: LCC PS3608.O482565 L58 2020 (print) | LCC PS3608.
O482565
(ebook) | DDC 811/.6--dc23
LC record available at https://lccn.loc.gov/2020024411
LC ebook record available at https://lccn.loc.gov/2020024412

10 9 8 7 6 5 4 3 2 1

All rights reserved. No portion of this book may be reproduced, stored in an
electronic retrieval system, or transmitted in any form or by any
means—electronic, mechanical,
photocopy, recording, or any
other—except for brief
quotations in printed reviews,
without the prior permission
of the publisher.

Published by Paraclete Press
Brewster, Massachusetts
www.paracletepress.com
Digitally printed

for my family, Mike, Caitlin, Connor, and Amanda
and
for my Beloved

CONTENTS

I.
EMERGE WINGED

Litany of Flights	3
On the Efficacy of a Prophet	4
On Adoring You	5
Via Negativa: Painted Ladies	6
The Breaking	7
Unexpected Wings	8
Preaching of the Birds	9
Gleanings	10
Autumn Vine	11
Over the Falls	12
His Emblem Over Me	13
Pantoum of the Tinderbox	14
California Match Girl	16
Earth on Fire	17
Angel of Dark and Fire	18
Rain Comes in the Fourth Year	20
Song of the Sown	22
Sacrament of Spring	23
Organic Ink	24
Some Bird Soaring	25

II.
LOFT THE BONES

Blood Feather	29
The Superfluous Hen	30
Movable Feast	31
Catch Us the Foxes	32
The Prison Angel	33
The Joy Tree	34
The Tilling of Dorothy Day	36
One Handful with Tranquility	37
Revelation	38

This is what it looks like	39
St. John of the Cross Addresses the Dark Ray	40
Penelope at Her Unweaving	41
The Prince Decides	43
The Language of Open	44
Cherith	46
The Eagle	47
Water-Walkers	48
Winter Shoots	49
Exodus	50
Nocturne	51

III.
SCALE THIS LIGHT

Via Negativa: Mourning Dove	55
Morning Star	56
The Color Ultramarine	57
The Eyes I Have Desired	58
Do you want to be well?	59
Good Fruit	60
Fusion	61
After Palm Sunday	62
There is One Splendor of the Sun	63
Paul, Citizen of Heaven	64
The Filling Tree	66
Pink Moment on Mulholland	68
Evidence of a Burning Bush	69
Absent Warning	70
The Deer	71
Drawn	72
Transmission	73
Torchlight	75
Pillar of Cloud, Pillar of Fire	76
Substance Theory	78

ACKNOWLEDGMENTS   81

She followed slowly, taking a long time,
as though there were some obstacle in the way;
and yet: as though, once it was overcome,
she would be beyond all walking, and would fly.
  —Rainer Maria Rilke, "Going Blind"

All burnt up, the soul renews like a phoenix . . .
  —Teresa of Avila, *Interior Castle*

I.

EMERGE WINGED

LITANY OF FLIGHTS

First, the winged movement, steady, forward. Scrub jays in flitting
progress, hawks in predator glide, a ringing up, a knife-sharp slope

down. Second, the effortless type, wind-splayed, motionless pinions
in thermal recline, as the Psalmist says, blessings breeze his love even

in sleep. Third, the hungry, against the gale, the destination singular
and the sun dipping crimson. Fourth, the metallic, business or pleasure.

Fifth, the whirring kind, all hummingbird. A picnic, apples and chocolate
in the garden with roses, both flower and child. You miss it when it's gone.

Sixth, a baffling flight of stairs, winding upward, passage and yet vehicle,
spiraling to unseen landings—hope courses in the kaleidoscopic lights.

Seventh, soar to the sun. Eighth, melt in bitter hubris. You know the story.
Ninth, escape. A flight out of Egypt, a path through the sea cleared by

divine hand. The times you ran, the times you were left behind in lament.
Tenth, only rotting in the belly of a whale tames your stubborn turn from

Nineveh. Eleventh, flights of despair and of yearning, two sides of one
letting go, hard-earned release back into the wild, unbound by expectation,

featherlike. Twelfth, in a moment, caught up high by the Beloved, the one
making all things work together, wings, body, arch, air—caught up, like the

Shulamite bride, to regions beyond aeronautical wisdom, transported in joy.
See, he says, the painful paring of your hollow bones has made you light.

ON THE EFFICACY OF A PROPHET

The ocean hushes and hums in my blood. The moon
takes up more of my eyes each night, swelling
sliver of revelation that turns and hides. What I want

to know is whether those luminous tendrils break
the surface. Why so fractional, this iridescence?
She brims and brims but cannot overflow. What

I suspect is this: the moon is a sibyl, whispers
what she does not fathom. She dresses in stolen
silk. She glides and foreshadows and slides away

at first hint of the eclipsing dazzle. What I see
glaringly: the sea rushes with every spray
of blue, green gleam of glass, break of cobalt,

bitter brine. The waters draw breath from the sun.
Yet the moon holds her tidal sway. Globes
of pearl take on the shimmer, waters pile high for her.

What I hear in the deep: she is royal messenger, gentle
ray, and what she speaks bends the burn, what she beams
flickers plunder, the little words of the sun I can bear.

ON ADORING YOU

In dark cords of night you weave for me
a cocoon of yourself. Splinters for silk,
thorns your thread, a love poured, an emptied
truth. I drink, in stripped unknowing. I long
to emerge winged, a bloom from black earth,
for love is stronger than death.

At sunrise you plait a pink-embered sky
with chattering towhees. Dew shines,
a needlework of mercy. Sugar maples
reach skyward, bud purple. You stitch
starlings, silvered chaparral, morning
glories, the faces I kiss—I feast
on the oranges of your love.

In strands mysterious I delight in you
in yet a third way. In the cellar under
silenced words, you wait, your impossible
wine in stone water jars. Golden threads
embrace, embroider, draw me,
astonished, to you.

VIA NEGATIVA: PAINTED LADIES

Unbound they float as if magnetized,
orange flurries pulled northwest,

born to discard chrysalis and thistle,
in fixated flight to the unknown;

they multiply, their number a migratory feast
in a year of want and ash. I have always felt safe

in your embrace. Yet I circle when I should fly
blind to the sun. Your spring hills

lead on to terraces of scarlet skyrocket
and hip-high mustard super bloom,

spreading a banquet in the sight of winter.
Buttercups, lupine blue wave me upcountry,

the light my road, the wind my release, my exodus
and compass you.

THE BREAKING

Perhaps transition resists the breaking;
the breaking up, the breaking down,
all the shattered bones of our being,

the fumbling to arrange jigsaw pieces
by lightness. The linger of the ache,
always biting at the elbow, inescapable

as your own shadow, dogging you except
in the brilliant noon blaze, when the pain
creeps unnoticed under moving feet.

Or maybe change craves the breaking,
the breaking out, the breaking away,
when all the stars join in perfect pitch,

the melody clear and silvered, spheres
breathing bright breaks in the night sky.
The seeping of steady light, the desert

spaces abloom with sudden fiddlenecks,
baby blue eyes, blinking open. The new
hawk chick spreads wobbly wings, learns

to hurl shadows to the ground below.

UNEXPECTED WINGS

Ninety-one degrees even as the sun flickers low,
my son stands tall, epicenter of buzzing children,
unruly excited bees to his sweet nectar: soccer.

They have little, but every week grow rich in runs,
breathless goals, high-fives, and him; even
before he gets out of the car they call his name.

They flock eagerly around him, try their feet at it,
kick, try again. A boy falls in facedown sprawl,
cries in the grass. My son kneels at his side, but he

will not stand. My son speaks soft words I cannot
hear, and I see his hand, patting the shaking back.
Someone near me says autistic, the child is autistic,

as if tears can be shut up neat and put away there.
The boy sits up suddenly, sobs I fail I fail I fail. I
cannot think who of us does not. My son coaxes

the boy onto trembling feet. And here is the thing,
my son keeps his hand on the boy's shoulder as
infinite moments tick by, and wherever he walks

on the field, the boy stays right next to him, under
his arm. The ball bumps, the kids zig and zag,
the sunset a gold whir of unexpected wings.

PREACHING OF THE BIRDS

Yesterday on the feast of St. Francis, I thought—if he were here,
preaching to the birds, wrapped in his tunic of everyday, his holy knees

would sink to my dying grass, one hand pressed to the rough breast
of Sister Earth, one lifted skyward in benediction of all flight.

The winged would settle quiet, content to roost and preen his every
word into each feather, so that later each golden note of courage

would lift, float under their hurtling bodies like afternoon
angels blowing updrafts, thermals of divine daring, contrails marking

the good fight, the hard business of shouldering onward, scraping
insects and droplets of water to nourish this fragile

life, the only one given, gives itself away, or is taken by others.
Violence snaps in the bushes, creeps at the edges

of the lawn, but Francis sits cross-legged in the center, his frayed
cloak breezed wide as a hawk as he lifts voice in fluid

melody, his chest expanding lyric, offers praise of the great
Goodness who reverberates new hum eternal, the one true warble

of leaf and sunshine and dew, of treetop and sky-tuned beak,
of peeping tufted bundles and sure first yellow shafts of day.

Everything else—here his notes crest higher, brush the blue
underskirt of eternity—everything else lies outside the light, outside

our soft nested peace. Today, full of his joy, their throats spilled over
his sermon to me, and I awoke unbound as those disciples of the air.

GLEANINGS

The apple pears weigh pink-gold, fall
    into fingers or grass. Gravity

summons them to their assignment. I
    pluck for my red wicker basket

yet leave fruit behind, gleanings
    (do not reap to the very edges)

drawing the little cottontails first, then
    emboldened squirrels

(leave them for the poor) next scrub jays
    and a roadrunner (and foreigners

residing among you). They browse together
    within inches, a menagerie

of pecking beaks and grappling paws,
    and peace. St. Francis would preach

but I watch from the window   let the quiet
    plenty expound on your love.

AUTUMN VINE

Where nothing grew, you planted your vine.
You prefer a plant that produces, you said,
one that climbs. The clusters

flourished: rust-stained green globes
crowd the vast vine, tart skins stretch
over sugary pulp. Under your watering can,

everything grows. What will happen when
the harvest comes, when the days shorten,
when the beads slide too quickly

through the fingers? Where will you plant,
what will you grow, in alien time zones
and seasons? The vine slants in autumn sun,

runs the distance of the trellis, tendrils reach
into space. The ripeness weighs, attracts ants,
scrub jays, looting squirrels. Yet I will not

pluck away the sweetness. Let your nearness
remain, let me remain in it, vats of joy
before the press of distance.

OVER THE FALLS

Breezing on the breath of God we trust to the edge,
sails brave with stirred spirit. We will rush
smooth in sun always, we think, the lapis sky
opens to fill us with theophany, honey
from the rock, bottomless oil jugs, kisses not clouds

yet thunder comes, blackness presses, we plummet
over the falls, a rushing vortex of dark confusion,
into freefall, chaos.

Shooting, merciless waterfall
rumbles, taunts: Now where
is your help? In the
crashing centrifuge
thoughts fracture, sink.

Hope grapples, shreds.
Losses mount, rocks
sharply   part our ways.
Once-graceful shapes
Shatter   into   jagged
shards of   self.

Velocity   grips,   twists
us away,   apart,   anew,
a shimmering, sure
splintering.   Love casts a
fearless   choice of
abandon,   overcoming
we plunge   into riverhead of
joy
rippling hearts now strangely, infinitely whole, a glint upon the waters,
home.

HIS EMBLEM OVER ME
Song of Songs 2:4, 5:6–7 — For Saint Teresa of Calcutta

Nowhere to lay your head,
nothing to call your own.
Why must it cost so much
to empty and to roam?

Holed up inside my heart
the stubborn will clings;
you turn out the precious pocket,
you bruise and break the seams.

Now, beloved, come to me,
I am wounded, dark, and blue—
your colors unfurl over me,
I suffer in search of you.

I wait in roiling silence,
but no hand is at the lock.
Only absence, empty holes,
and smashing on the rock.

Am I not your cherished bride?
Yet I am abandoned, lost.
Your neglect I hide; I smile, I
wear the poverty of your cross.

Nowhere to lay my head
makes me yet your own;
nothing save imprint of you
on yielded heart, our home.

PANTOUM OF THE TINDERBOX

Even now you could send a drop
For the beating box of my brittle heart
Years now so dry, no rain, no refrain
Your lush green melody hushed away

From the beating box of my brittle heart
You hide in shifting scorched sand
Lush green melody a hushed memory
I wander this, your parched desert

You hide in searing scorched sand
My charred lips crack, peel in pain
I wander this, your parched desert
My throat rattles stripped prayer

My charred lips crack, appeal in vain
Fingers twist like dying vines
My throat rattles, stripped of prayer
Once verdant land crumbles to stubble

Fingers twist like dying vines
You say only, "I want it dry"
My verdant land crumbles to stubble
Again: "I am building a fire in you."

You say only, "I want it dry"
So dry all my bones ache and cry
Again: "I am building a fire in you."
Drought presses on within, without

So dry all my bones ache to cry:
Strike up the lightning march, then!
Drought presses on within, without
St. John tells me you are living fire

Strike the lightning match, then!
Your gasping, arid box awaits
St. John tells me you are loving fire
Turn tinder to bright ardent flame

Your gasping, arid box awaits
Years now so dry, no rain, no refrain
Turn tender, ignite ardent flame
Even now you could drop the match.

CALIFORNIA MATCH GIRL

It's combustible here, where humidity
thins and the wind howls. Parched

the gusting pepper trees, unsuspicious
kindling the peopled homes, too ready

to bloom in flame. We brush cut,
we arson watch, we red flag but really

we just hope the witch does not shove us
into the seething oven and slam the door hard.

We don't expect it until the billow of acrid
smoke already chokes our lungs. We simmer

just outside the smoldering edges of our volatile
vulnerability, oh so fireproof.

Striking matches to see the starry vision, biting
into the shiny red apple, pricking innocent

fingers on the spindle, falling down the hill, off
the wall, into the well, down the beanstalk,

beating the giant against all odds by sheer grace.
A woman told me that after the fire her house

stood alone in the stark landscape, charred inside.
Near the fireplace, sucked down the chimney

in the midst of the firestorm, left among the cinders
she found a half-burned page from a children's book,

not belonging to her. She could not make out
which story, but we all know it.

EARTH ON FIRE

A haze of smoke hangs high, a red-eyed
canopy of uncertain danger, strange, yet more
and more familiar with each passing news cycle,
as day follows brittle day. Drought has pressed

grass into crunchy brown scrub, plum trees into
tinder, heartbeats of the phoebe into a clattering
for water, seed, relief. Yet what comes is fire, relentless
inferno, licking red tongues of destruction, flames

clasping hands with scorching sirocco winds,
outstripping jackrabbits, incinerating chaparral,
walnuts, oaks, all one in the blazing terror of wild,
consuming hunger. The wisdom of birds grows silent.

(Yet, did you not say you came to set the earth on fire?)

Now listen to what was left behind. The very soil lies
coal black, hills turned to ash, to nothing; every contour
bared in mourning, broken only by harsh bony fingers of
ebony oak corpse, stabbing through the side of moonscape.

(Yet, did you not say you wished it were already blazing?)

Let me tell you what I see there, on the shoulders
of the charred foothills. What was fire, and death, and
the end, has become a new Jerusalem. She is shadowed
yet beautiful. She says, "Do not stare at me because

I am dark, because living fire has burned me." What
flames have turned ash, the beloved embraces. What
lies barren births anew, a shared, open heart, suffering
yet transformed, transforming, still in bride-clothes.

A seed lies there, one that only knows to break open
at the caress of its natural mother, fire.

ANGEL OF DARK AND FIRE

My angel most certainly
dwells in darkness and fire.
She my assigned warrior
battles night and chaos.

She lives in the crags
between asleep and awake.
Sword glinting, eyes
a steely might in my favor.

Born fire from Fire
she is of the Fire I love.
You, set in my heart,
set as a seal, burning.

You encircle me, you
make flame her buckler.
Why should I fear?
She prevails, powerful
sentry in this world; yet
she dissolves, forceful
magnet to the next.

Darkness is yet light
in that kingdom.
A temporary blindness
which opens wide.

My angel stands in
divine darkness,
the black hole of
her unseen weight
compels, urges me
into lightness,
a surrender to brightness.

In her there is no fear.
I long for such wings.
Reaching sightless
my embrace meets
the alchemy of
your Fire. Cares forgotten,
I take flight.

RAIN COMES IN THE FOURTH YEAR

Drought-flamed leaves wake
in bewilderment under
the unfamiliar caress of
liquid mercy,
a strange drenching of hope.

Sugar maple fingers drip
myrrh, precious dew;
persimmons gather courage,
gasping pepper trees and
wasting cottontails revive.

Roots remember
Elijah casting prayer
over the sea long ago;
changed hearts
watered the dust of Carmel.

Every living thing
drinks, colors deepen,
darken with wet blessing.
The collective breath draws damp,
sighs relief.

At last you have turned your face
to us, wreathed in cloud.
Your gentle rain
quiet as the prayer
of our very cells.

And the towhees and larks,
darting acrobats
in air washed
clean
of the dry multitude of regrets,
pierce the sky with
reaching cascades of joy.

SONG OF THE SOWN

Who is the seedling heartbeat of the tree?
You were, and are, and ever shall be;
Yet, she-who-is-not also might come to be—
In muddy, graced intertwine of root and leaf.

Deep within, she winds and waits,
Close in the kernel's embrace;
Deep without, horizonless yield,
Sheaves, glinting crown of run race.

Yet between; ah, the joyful, painful between
Of simply with—a disintegrating unity
As sown seed gives over self to sod—*Selah*
And becomes green unfolding we.

SACRAMENT OF SPRING

Heavy with hibernation and eye-blink, I
flatten dewy baby green blades. I wonder
why my silver-tipped bear hair belongs here

in the glorious garden of fresh bursting pear
blossoms, where even branches birth red tender
shoots, newborn fists opening in innocent

praise. *Light and rain and life!* they cry, reach
to suckle sunshine. My hip scoffs, grumbles
an unwelcome antiphon. *But you too*, whisper

a thousand verdant buds on rejoicing hills
—*you too!* Fragrant roses draw, tumble me
on knees in invitation to inhale incense,

cinnamon crescendo, cardamom of angels.
Goldfinches swell the song—*You too too too.*
You new new new. Sight and sound and

scent of the sacrament of spring surge into
my heart, a living lightning strike of joy, kiss
electric, sparking blooms unknown to begin.

ORGANIC INK

Petals unfold from your tongue, you speak crimson
velvet freshness into being. An opening bud of careful
precision, a floral life floating on your breath, bees, and boundary.

You expand a mystery of molecules, at your word atomic spice
springs into breeze; you dizzy hummingbirds, intoxicate butterflies.
Shining beams play, shimmer, light your Shulamite, invite a tango.

You draw. Come, find my notes poured out in the garden, etched among
lemons and limes. See, the lost apricot awakens! Sweet shoots adorn
black crumbling branches. On every cell I inscribe: what was dead is alive.

You wait for me to discover your love among the leaves and thorns,
(will I perceive it?) your hidden blossom of wonder, a shy heart-shaped
valentine of third heaven, a sachet for this moment, a marked downbeat

of song, a bodily inhale of my eyes and skin and hair and breath. Filled
with rising melody, your unspoken lyrics whispered on wind, I join
your written roses in swaying dance, in blood-red bloom of belonging.

SOME BIRD SOARING

Things are falling away
steadily under
the chisel
of Michelangelo's creator.

Slabs of alabaster self
pain, crash, pile.
Who knew I did not need
such cold weight?

Bittersweet
    but finely balanced.

Pared away
    but smooth and light.

Inscribed
    yet gliding free.

A sharper silhouette.

Translucent wings
flex, honed hawk
thin to let the sun
shine through.

A traveler squints
against the glare,
seeking direction,
a chart for change.
There:

some bird, soaring!

Her face glows.

I leave it to her
to puzzle out
the markings.

I just fly.

II.

LOFT THE BONES

BLOOD FEATHER

The critical feathers number primary one
through ten. The blood and the feathers

beat, loft the bones, out-maneuver attack,
carry life. The plan to reintroduce

a healthy red-tail into the wild
to take his natural swift talon-hold

banked sharply with a sudden blood
feather, a jagged splintering of primary

three, the largest flight feather, bleeding
profusely pleading for a stop

with a homemade flour remedy, tender
fingers to patch the hurt. Avian

blood, like a body driven by love,
refuses to coagulate, would rather die

than gather itself, slow the rushing
red pursuit, turn and solidify alone.

THE SUPERFLUOUS HEN

How my heart pricks with green tender envy
of SFO airport. Her unseeing monitors gaze
on the dear cheeks and chins of my chicks,

the absent treasures my eyes seek hungrily,
haggard on camera-caught smiles, fading in
the hall. She has the real sunshine, flooding

the chambers of her lifeless heart, an empty
incubation. Once I gathered my darlings
under my wings, snug among these words,

a naughty bunny, a kind collie-dog, a clever
fox. Jemima Puddle-duck, who could not sit
her own eggs to hatching, complained of she

who could, the superfluous hen. Each vowel
careful, warble the syllables, twist of tongue,
kissed into ears—sü-ˈpər-flü-əs. Melodious

grain, nibbled. You will fly one day, all golden
feathers, buoyed on my adoring, I thought. But
the distances increased, my pinions cannot reach

Philly, to rowboats on sparkling East Coast lakes,
nor Chicago Orchestra Hall, hushed to hear their
soaring song. Now they line up, eager, stretching

under metallic wings at SFO, and I, chickless,
absurd as Jemima, lament the superfluous hen.

MOVABLE FEAST

I want to give you the cardinal Christmas ornament
in the shop, the one with snow-dusted feathers
and sparkly eyes   also the auburn fox stretched

in flight flecked with glitter. I want to give you all
the dishes of the menagerie, prickly hedgehogs,
shy rabbits, proud zebras with arched backs,

hummingbirds floating, surprised   also the cups
rimmed round in shining gold, so that you eat
and drink of me and my love. I want to pluck

the birdsong from the morning sky and wrap it
for you, in swaths of sunlight   festooned in
silver-edged bands of blue heaven. I want to mix

honey with lemons cut in tiny tangy pieces
and give you all the tea   all the teapots also, clay
and porcelain, and stacks and stacks of hours to savor

every sweet steeped amber drop. I want to give you
crimson-draped sugar maples   each still-tender leaf
flaming with love, alight in the dance of adoring

your heart. I want to give you all the bowls of fragrant
prayers, all the fingers clasped in thanksgiving, all
the vowels of praise   ascending, all the joy in the

halls of light, and also in the halls of darkness, among
the little sparrows gazing so faithfully at your cloak of cloud.
I want to write my life   on a sheet of linen paper

spill all the notes of my love, from first dawn to dawnless day:
the pounding lament, the soaring victory, the hushed longing,
and give it to you.

But you have already given it all to me.

CATCH US THE FOXES

In the silvery shadow of
All Hallows Eve
you appeared, blue fox.

(Catch us the foxes, beloved.
Their teeth cut sharp on the vines.)

You crush moonflowers,
spoil with careless mouth.
You prefer the struggle of
a sparrow to her flight.

(Their teeth cut sharp on the vines.)

Nimble feet so quick to
run away forever without
the wink of a farewell.

(Catch us the foxes, the little foxes
that damage the vineyards.)

Your proud shrub of a tail—
trailing, yet governing.
You never knew yourself.

(They damage the vineyards, and
our vineyards are in bloom!)

Less blue fox than ghost,
you stared frozen in my light,
abandoned your place, a vapor
vanishing into the chill dark,
a specter among specters.

And our vineyards bloom sweet
in the sun.

THE PRISON ANGEL
For Mary Clarke Brenner, Mother Antonia of La Mesa Prison of Tijuana

The Beverly Hills home empties of children, husbands,
blonde dims gray, you wonder
if you missed the turn.

Your hope wears jesses, caught tight
in the glove of disappointment.
Even unbound, it looks for the gauntlet.

Affliction, it is said,
produces endurance produces
proven character
        produces
hope   and as hope
does not disappoint,
it cannot be contained in the fist.

Twice divorced, at the age of fifty
you stitch a veil, find
liberty in the cell of a Tijuana prison.

You coax convicts, fend off fights. You feed,
nurse, forgive them. Five foot two inches,
you stop fires and bullets and hostage-taking in a riot.

You turn their hearts, you wear the cross
they form for you of nails and copper wire.
Madre a los hijos.

Thirty years jailed, what you release
makes you radiant. What you hold flies free.

THE JOY TREE

Her dragon scales startle, a bark of cutting thorn.
As a tender sapling, sharp green exclamation points
warned the world of her self-containment. Now
time-thick and wise, her silver spikes declare:
She has other food of which you know not.

Silk-Floss stretches, reaches high, traces flight
of falcons. She aches to soar, burst bloom but knows
the irony of her name; bristles rip silk, barbs belie
angels. Needles prick, but the finches do not mind.

In spring, woody whorls of hope ring round inside.
She ponders the parade of daffodils, irises, azaleas.
Lilies unveil, daisies lift sunny heads. Boxwoods
bud, swallowtails sail through her fingers.

Summer boasts asters, roses, marigolds, blue sugar
berries. Jacarandas pop purple, birds of paradise
sing her to sleep on wafting spice. Peaches glow
like young dashing suns, globes of juicy promise.

Still she waits. Her thorns reveal her difficulty,
a passion out of season, empty. No warm budding
petals for her, no opening peals of mirth. Yet beneath
the spines her sap runs sure, sweet, ticks out her time.
She knows her creator knows his creation.

Autumn chills her roots. Persimmons catch gold fire.
Others flutter candy apple, butter, ginger. No show
of scarlet silk for her. She grimaces, groans, drops
her drab downcast leaves. It is finished.
And who would have thought any more of her?

Winter breaks, she wakes bright, shocks the sparrows.
Scrub jays scream, squirrels stare. In the gloom she
blushes pink blossoms, stands unfolded, complete.
Her limbs dazzle, robed in radiance. In the darkness
of the barren month, undisturbed in patient longing,
she reaches full flower of love—joy.

THE TILLING OF DOROTHY DAY

Her swollen hands red in peeling service, dutifully brooming
the floor beneath his feet, beneath his spitting, his foul words,

yellowed eyes, beneath his stench and snaking abusive stare;
his crusted lips, crowded with curses, at last goad apart her own.

All the work for the Worker, all the suffering for the Suffering,
all the poverty for the Poor, all the anguish for the Anguished,

stacked high, combusting in angry flare of exhaustion, frustration
crucifixion. She opens her mouth hotly.   Sudden

as a silver shaft of sun piercing the dim cloud she sees a dazzling
face, a mountain unsuspected, even doubted, now shimmering clear,

though the rest of the land still sits sullen in dank purpled shadow:
St. Thérèse of Lisieux appears between her and the man. Smiling.

So startled, her unspoken vitriol flies hastily to the mountain on
the thrust of that unveiled mildness. So reminded, her mouth falls silent.

Even when the vision shutters, the scent of roses remains. Even
when the fragrance fades, the flower sinks sturdy roots down inside.

Even when she turns now, broom in hand, she feels the Mercy bloom.

ONE HANDFUL WITH TRANQUILITY

The time of April ticks onward outside, on the hills, in the chaparral,
under sagebrush, an awakening from the ashes and the barren ache.

The swallows return, an aerial army swooping to reclaim terrain,
the muddy need to nest pulsing in their blood. The rushing, rustling

fight for the safety of the eaves, a time to build: our own daily lot.
A scrub jay works the red roses, mounts his throne among thorns,

hop-foots to beak a beetle prize. Paired woodpeckers parent noisily,
the tiny subjects of their reverberating anxiety tucked, fed, hidden.

The earth exhales scented afternoon breeze, electric sweet and seeded
with urgent life and urge to life throbbing in the wings, a time

to be born, the buds bursting pink, the fresh blades of grass pushing,
pushing up, a time to plant, the children growing, growing strong.

The darkness underneath, the clay knowledge of endings inevitable,
gives over to beginnings, the springing up of greenness and wild

heaven-blue lupine blooms crowning the scorched knoll, lilacs,
lavender, bellflowers, poppies announce a time of fragrant plenty.

This is mercy, this forgetting of the winter, the drought, the fire, and
the hunger; the shuddering deep of the sigh, a time to release, a time

to love, come what may. This is mercy, this forgetting to remember,
the remembering to forget all except now, this present, this presence.

REVELATION

Last night did you see the lightning,
like silvered bolts in a basin of
purple cloud? No thunder at all,

she says, only shards of light.
I made her drive me up to the top
of the mountain, just to watch.

Here she turns to her sister,
smile answering smile.
God is in everything,

everywhere I look; this morning
in the swallowtail out of nowhere.
Her quiet words flutter and fold.

I am fluent in her tongue,
the faith-embered flash in her eyes.
Those bowls filled with electricity

in turn become my divine lightning;
there also alights his sudden butterfly:
in the easy love between two sisters

his wings open bright.

THIS IS WHAT IT LOOKS LIKE

when the fiery chariots of the sugar maple rush
sky high, when their mama's candle flames out, gray

winter-bared trunk like an aimless wraith. The one
who gave, burst out in buds, cradled her cleaving

shoots. The one who watered her sprouts, rain
or no rain, each rustling moment a feast. The one now

nakedly windswept. February hearts have come
and gone, been put away in the cardboard box. Who

will the cupids come out for, now that her little fires
have taken leave, like Elijah gone in a blazing

red swirl, matured, assured, caught up, flying
away, broken away from her branches, fluttering soft

goodbyes, thrilling to what comes next. In their wake,
this is what it looks like, cold bark stripped smooth,

roots holding earth, boughs holding nothing at all.

ST. JOHN OF THE CROSS ADDRESSES THE DARK RAY

Dark
flame burning
I know you are there
by the unbearable heat,
the blackened walls.
Your work is never done,
you return day by day, night
by dark night, incinerating me with love.
The peeling of the petalled persona, shedding
of the skins, the luminous sheath sloughed,
a blistered shell hissing in
the blaze of your furnace. I long for the fire of you there
in the not-there. Your hidden face breaks down the
blast door, drags the wormed wood by the splinters
into your white-hot perfection: an agony. Who can see your face
and live? Why are your features branded in the landscape
of my heart, a seal recognized in the conflagration?
There is no other place for us to go, Lord. You speak the flames
of everlasting life. Come then, smolder to ash the wrong turns,
the brazen affronts, the buried mistakes, catch them
into bright storms of embered hope. You give your tender
love thus: inferno-bright blade finding the midpoint of
something beyond words in the birth of me, in the core of me,
in the sweet smarting center of my spilled-over swooning
soul. You smelt, form resplendent light;
melting, I can only shine in liquid joy, can only leap like
candlelight, can only become, at your touch,
dark flame burning.

PENELOPE AT HER UNWEAVING

I feel it coming like a welting bruise, a purple
tentacle of cloud, high tide. How naïve to believe

the castle would stand. Our sandy words
carved rooms only we knew, a moat

to keep us safe, the rhythmic rushing in
and out of the very thing that would erode

the golden bones of the palace we
made together. Salt-drenched

years falter, in your absence suitors slaver
my shuttle stammers, unravels, dumbly

speaking the damage. You paid a traveling potter
to throw a bowl for me, the glaze hardened

into the swirling green and gray glimmers
of a winter sky. I could never take a spoon

to the pretty vessel you left behind
to feed me. It gleams its distant glints

and starves me. I feel it coming like a vision,
déjà vu of dark washing waves of grief that crest

with the moon, particles of what was firm drifting
in the sea, separated and meaningless

in the separation, the castle once, now shattered
scattered motes moving with the flick of a fishy

tail. Leagues and shipwrecks and continents apart,
suspended in the very thing that destroyed us.

The drowning all dream my dream: a turn
of tide between us, a windswept beach, a clean

start. A fevered hope to awaken to the dream,
carried home by the very thing that can save us.

THE PRINCE DECIDES

Everything points to you today, rose. The sun above, the seeds below,
the sheep, in his crinkled paper box, this desert landscape of loneliness.

All the questions exploding in my chest spring from my distant planet,
they all sink their roots in you. Inquisitive sprouts grow into unruly

unasked brush, burning in fiery tangles, a baobab unintended, neglected
thicket of sharp briar longing. Questions I must ask, demand, repeat:

What did you reveal? Love. What did you mean by it? Love.
What can I possibly do, now that I quit you with such decisive action,

a leaving I was bound to commit, now birthing unnaturally, unexpectedly
a yearning to return that yields not, a force erupting in silence. A volcano

untended tends to blow. If only I had cleaned it carefully, acknowledged
the contents of my crestfallen crater I might have learned it on my own.

Now I seek, call to you in thought and word and question and musing,
love tended only within myself, not tendered
to you in tending what
I tamed and
tamed me.

You call, unspeaking, from taproot to closed eye of petal, mysterion,
an inexorable pull vibrating each heartstring tremolando, wind on

winter wheat. Love flashes out like an uncoiling snake, irrefutable
seismic wave, my answer at last to you, my fragrant earthquake:
gravity

reversed
homing to you,
my singular bloom among the stars.

THE LANGUAGE OF OPEN

At the very center, pistil to petal
you remain in my rose, all fragrance.
You are honey and lemons in my tea.
I know your knock on my whittled-down
hut of abandonment, abode of withered hope,
the disappointed country, cut hard to stubble.

The language of open is not spoken here, but
one of a bitter kind, biting, not abiding.
You know your knock on the black uneven
timber of my last door, the one I cannot see,
the one built by those neglectful architects
the grasshoppers, when I wanted, oh, I wanted
                                      the butterflies.

I know your knock, you know my wooden knot
the hurt resistance, a sullen swelling silence.
You subdue, you submerge with your peace,
honeyed fingers and citrus smile, balm of Gilead.

So much adoring poured out, overflowing my
teacup, my acorn of anguish, the very universe
brought to bear, to touch, to hold, to cure my cold,
to coax apart, to warm, delight, to cross over a
forbidding threshold with rush of winged light.
                                    Unweighted, I forget.

Honeybee gold in the glow of coming free,
my petals reach wide, soak sunshine
unfurl the incense of an answer, open
the drawbridge, spilling out one short
syllable of surprised dawnbreak,
surrendering the lot, joying in loss,
flaming into the splendid bloom of yes.

CHERITH

Before you sent me down to the wadi there was
that goldfinch, shining.
swaying, it lingered   warbled, flew away,
away   away to the blue mountain, each beat of wing
a stop in my heart—stay
stay, stay   the shadow of your bird
in me shifted, my love slipped the green and lilac
banks of the river, beyond rushes and the reaches
of my throat.

Then those days wheeled on the track, puffing,
mechanical and drawn. A thousand tongues choked
on salt, not bread. I turned, turned into a pillar looking
for your warm yellow breast.

A drought later I forgot to remember, how you had taken
yourself away from me   my reshaped heart steadied,
bundles and branches worn into grooves, patience
uncounted.

Is that why you sent me down to Cherith, to hide me
in your hands, to drink of the stream in cool deep swallows?
sometimes I am afraid to touch the beauty of the emerald
mossy stones, they make me ache with riparian joy

Your goldfinches alight, feed me presence and song, and it is for
this your finest wheat   I have longed.

THE EAGLE

I cannot look at the sky the day of your funeral   crying down
rain, rivering into your open grave. Although he will never walk

the earth again, the priest intones. Mud shrouds my shoes, no upper
visible. In the church the panes reach for heaven   but that glass

cuts far above me. Mouths scatter stories like ashes, fingers tap me,
Did you see? The eagle in the window? Floating   while we sang

"On Eagle's Wings," rising up to the steeple on cue? My cousin:
Did you? The eagle?   He will never walk the earth again.

For years I refused the eagle   that was not my own because I
did not see.   If a tree falls, and you do not hear the breaking,

does it truly?   hints of a toppled trunk, of a feathered miracle
muscle against open eyes and the hard heartwing beat of sorrow.

The logic of grief instructs: absence is a bitter remainder. Holes
blacken with weight, nothingness augments, an ironic gravity

multiplier.   Seventeen years later it came to me,
the divine point: the cloud rather than the ray. The things hoped

rather than grasped. The unheard pine cracks, and the fissures run
through me, the golden glides outside the frame, beyond my sight,

and wings thrust in my blood that keeps pumping, pumping forward,
my holed tongue tasting the way home. Perhaps you do not walk,

my father, in fields I cannot know. Yet, the tree.   The eagle.

WATER-WALKERS

The particular value of a curl of brown leaf you find
hard to explain. Autumn-dropped, in the pool

of your wading, cooling the limbs as you immerse
and swirl in matters which may be otherwise.

How to explain that it is really not about the leaf,
which glides languorous toward destruction

surely in the filter by morning sodden and fallen into
fragments, dissolving into not-leaf. No, the secret drifts

across the bottom, the step, the wall, tumbles in silence
for you—only you—to see, a shadowed telegraph,

a shaped shade of heart. The curve of the veined skin
will soften in its sinking, take on the heavy water

capsize in the course of things, the usual course
run by leaves, by upside-down bees, by spiraling

seed-pods, by all us water-walkers. The curve points
in transience, doubled. The sliding perfect heart

cast below resembles it not, yet leaf and sunlight
water and breeze conspire to utter a message of hope

in the not-hope. The stem shadow a shank of weightless
anchor: may you float light, fasten dark to the bedrock.

WINTER SHOOTS

In hailstorm of sightless swirl, the chaos close,
closer, you separate the light from the dark, you
reveal a part of you, a spark in me, a tender green

pod of peace, pearl of great price, here within, quiet.
Peace or pea or pearl, clasped in cloistered hiding,
cloaked yet shining. She speaks courage to me: look

to my new swelling verdant belly, not the dark lands.
Those decay, they fall away, but this remains, this anchor
of future, not past. You lament calendar and clock, you

open gates to flood, you usher away hope like an empty-
eyed mourner. But see here—lush tranquility! Promise
endures here, tucked secure, sowed. It will not disappoint.

Even beneath your notice (notice how you do not notice),
the upsurging growth, the bursting fruit, perfect out of
imperfect, fertile out of futile, mysterious globe of seed

stirs awake, a hardborn faith, planted all along, sprouting
in the season of hollowed heartbeat—vision of victory,
gazing straight at night, breathing sweet, budding, climbing.

EXODUS

Was it shining tunnel or crimson crawlway,
curve of salty side dripping shaft of Egyptian sun refracted as they
unfurled in frantic flight eyes closed against drowning?

I am vastly empty so lonely now he is gone.
The pink of my cheek wet the furrows white with anguish.
The parting of the waves a vise-cracking of the heart

ribs open to the sky. Bleeding out is not what a body expects.
My Osiria roses, licks of flame scrolling inward to ash
the life-blood pulses, fragrant offering up to transfigured glow.

The waters saw you, beloved. They trembled through their hips,
you opened wide the red mouth and hummed us home.
Let us pass through the parting part us in passing, it happens that way.

Only part of me is sure of the dividing path but yes I am
sure of the yes, the ruby passage of you, splendid sea, lodestar,
undertow pulling me beyond reach, through your tangled deep,

navigation belonging only to my belonging to you.
Those Osiris buds of life of death of life after death
of flood-plain arching with birth of Nile-ripped dust.

Let us drink what laps at the root split and start the bloom.

NOCTURNE

Silk of a thousand shades flows from your throat, night
notes billow, float, dance in the sleeping garden, tangle
of rosebush the shadowed lectern of your liturgy. Star
beams cannot find your gray body but fiery sparks issue

from open beak: scrub jay shriek melts into lilt of robin,
goldfinch warble sharpens to hawk cry, hoot owl, medley
of sky and tree. You wing wide, embrace all nations of the
tongue, a writer of icons, singing doorways of egg and gold

and open eyes, a call to the soaring beyond. You chant the
quilt of creation, hymn to fingers that wove the fabric of
melody, conducted patterns of feather, flight and fugue.
Now the phoebe's sweet chirp, swallow's chatter, scraping

crow-caw, you swallow the wide world whole just to croon
your divine office, embroider blessing on the hours, lauds
in blackness. Mockingbird, you settle on my chimney top
like a church steeple, trilling frogsong, the cricket's hum,

burbling laugh of the neighbor child. You chat, you rasp,
chirrup, scold. You sing sunlight in the darkness, telling
cocoons and keening coyotes how we were knitted to love,
endure, and even in the cleft of night, joy in spilling praise.

III.

SCALE THIS LIGHT

VIA NEGATIVA: MOURNING DOVE

Sightless in morning fog,
she laces fallen fibers

of fan palm, bunchgrass,
the birch's lost twigs,

spins an empty creation.
Conifer needles, the fox's hair

round out the void,
what was cast off and left

for dead now the dwelling,
twined with stippled space

of eggs to come, primeval
point of departure, dawn

chorus chipping the dark.
Wings rustle, expand

the hollow, nothing
yet something, expectant.

MORNING STAR

Stirring first as slight ripple
that expands
in unison true, the opening
of the mouth, a word spoken.

Breath and breeze gather
against the heavy warp
shoving, shifting until the boom
judders a new bearing.

An exhale, then movement,
the water slides beneath. We
stay up all night looking for the stars,
less cosmic compass than pinpricks
in the heart, prophets linking arms
with apostles, a body.

I teach you to prevail, you say, *I
light the way.*

We surrender the night-bound lamps,
clutch his shimmering words.
We make of ourselves
a tent for the sun.

THE COLOR ULTRAMARINE

a hue beyond   its own shores, the color of *for*
and *ever*, of longing   of portal,
a wave gathering,   swelling in unseen depth,

singlehearted. Beyond tide, ocean, this world,
beyond   blued teeth of the conch,
pulse of surf   of salt and vein.

The cerulean rim of horizon, the boundary
between us, yet   celestial riptides
carry me   closer. So precise, your particle

and wave   crest and trough, spectrum
in the aqua spray   in marine glow
of deep. The color of aliveness,   of gaze

from afar,   of washing with tears. Of being
known. Of diving   and swimming in circles.
A blue flame   in my soul, electric. Set me

as a seal   on the sky of your arm, lift me
into belonging. You know   the sapphire vaults
below and above   you know where to find

me, in amplitude   infinite   and ultra
finite   lapis lazuli crushed.   Take
the measure of my breaths   rushing in

and out, breakers   build and crash. If only
I could sprint this sea, scale   this light
saturated   blue my passage to you.

THE EYES I HAVE DESIRED

O spring like crystal! / If only, on your silvered-over faces, / you would suddenly form / the eyes I have desired, / which I bear sketched deep within my heart.
—John of the Cross, "The Spiritual Canticle"

Like a bride I walk upon petals,
cobalt florets kiss my arms as they

tumble, soft stars beneath my feet.
Panicles of lavender dot perfect above

in jacaranda and sky, Ezekiel's
sapphire throne of God glints,

cirrus angels touch leaden angles of
horizon. Scrub jays call, arrow azure.

All this falling down from heaven, so
fleeting, yet my momentary eyes

meet firmament, the unmoved
moving intensity of blue gaze.

For one long caught breath, even the hawks
swing down for me.

DO YOU WANT TO BE WELL?

he asks. Seems like a simple question

the man lies in a roughshod portico in Jerusalem
at the edge of the healing pool of Bethesda,
sick for thirty-eight years.

Was the inquiry ironic? Emphasis on *want*?

Can you blame the man for being
a little defensive, maybe you

or I also would start telling Jesus about how

we do not have,
    how no one helps,
        how we cannot move,
            how everybody else
                gets there first.
                    See this paralyzing
                    weight of flesh,
              these problems,
           these people,
        rooting me motionless
      even in the presence
of the divine cure.

But then that pointed question reduces
                    cuts through the noise, brings

the excuses boomeranging home:
Do you want to be well?

GOOD FRUIT

Children of Eve, are we free now? Or does the fruit,
once consumed, consume us still? All these mornings after

gnawing at the core, are *we* gnawed at the core, known
for our knowing, lost to a wholeness lying somewhere west

of our hunger, somewhere long excised in our memory,
but desired in our flesh, our cells homing to an Eden

like serpent-stung pushovers pining in a strange land?
By all rights the tree should bear no apricots, decayed

half-corpse, all broken sagging arms and knobby elbows,
the brittleness longing for the sap of youth, her maidenhood

quickened at the dawn of the world, up from a rib her roots.
She grew strong, smooth; her fruit burst golden sweetness.

A shimmering spider strand crosses her wrecked branches,
catches silver in the morning sun, arrows bright toward

impossible leaves greening, orbs of yellow ripening. Her side
splits with spark irrepressible, mother of the living again.

Her divided body forms one being. Children of Eve, despite
our fruit, do we all house deadness? Or despite all failure,

might we glint good light, push on to green, to gold?

FUSION
After Salvador Dali's Christ of Saint John of the Cross

1.
Uncrucified arms a sculpted triangle,
not-thorns a crown of chestnut hair,
splendid. The light of the world, head

bowed, radiates. The pigments flare,
suffuse gold fire:
he cannot be dimmed.

2.
John of the Cross, the friar of fire,
in love with the living flame of love
prayed to be a bonfire

of this Light. Unreservedly he selects
this angle, a wick of a man longing
for his lightning strike.

3.
In Dali's cosmic dream, Christ
blazes as the nucleus of the universe,
a moment which bears all,

scintillating atoms caught under
the brush, a death reversed by creator.
Gaze on him, resplendent, join

these your atoms to his, and ignite.

AFTER PALM SUNDAY

Led away to your passion, you said: if
this is what happens when the wood is green,
what will happen when it is dry?

What will happen? The flames
will take hold of the roof. The spire,
an architectural masterpiece,

will become a firework, the structure
exploding, shattering into pieces, the cross
tumbling into the nave like a sparkler.

The faithful will stand by and sing canticles
that will break your heart, they will sing
prayers for their Church on fire.

The roof and spire will incinerate, the blaze
so hot that the wood is consumed
before it can litter the cathedral floor.

What exalts itself will combust
and collapse, but the main structure,
the foundation, the stone—you will remain.

THERE IS ONE SPLENDOR OF THE SUN
1 Corinthians 15:41; 2 Corinthians 4:10

the moon holds another brightness, a bare seed caressed
by fire-clothed luminosity,
      lighting the glass darkly, a half-veiled face,

like half the body of fire-scorched acacia, Icarus-cracked
crepe leaves of lunar glint,
      half the body alight in sun, a shining green

humility, budding fresh, an untouched life. We too always
carry about such celestial
      half-lidded brilliance, a body chiaroscuro,

the dying of Jesus, so that our uncrucified lives show out,
leafy laughing crown still
      anchored branch, trunk, root, deep in soil,

a blackness musky with moondark, loam of the longing night.
One needs the other.
      His star fell down and dimmed for us,

to spark our candles awake, to flame alive molecules, shoots
from the shimmering vine.
      An eclipse serves well to darken us,

a reflecting body only, moon carrying about in it the lantern,
lightning in a bottle,
      splendor borrowed   yet burning in the body of the living.

PAUL, CITIZEN OF HEAVEN
Philippians 3:19–21; 1 Corinthians 15:37

In gravity dark, the worm discordant,
insects click syllables empty
of meaning. This maw of earth

moans of vanity, greed, oppression,
an upside-down grayscale of rot,
blind eyes and mole claws, digging,

an inverse glory of waste. I, alien,
am outcast, a sorrow   dying
yet living   a joy, belonging

to a place of light and winged song,
I cannot say where   but you hear
the thrum also, the seeded melody

of sweet words in the sown,
lightning across   the universe.
I see us rise, sisters and brothers,

roses, angel trumpets, star-gazers,
wreath of the body, unstoppably fragrant.
Gold glimmers above   I squint

through the clay   I strain upward
muddied of earth, but no citizen of earth.
I learn to love this loam of home

away from home   my dissolving station
reveals his germination, bare kernel opens
wide   narrows into a death like his. I

unfurl   gazing, naturalized,
found in you, new green I break
ground, my bloom the image your image

images in me   all along I was yours.

THE FILLING TREE

Corner gas station, snaked with dusty cars
slaking thirst, owners just as parched.
It's Sunday but everyone is looking down, away,

distant from the low-slung concrete walls,
the wafting petroleum fumes, the rumbling
throaty trucks, and VW Bugs with curled lashes.

Next door, if you look over, sits a drab house
with antennae, perched tight as an insect.
On its desiccated patch of yard, bang

against the peeling concrete wall, rises
an astonishing coral tree. If you're looking,
you blink twice, check to see if you are wearing

your rose-tinted sunglasses, but no,
you left them in the driver's seat. You marvel
at the red. It's not fire-engine, nor some lurid logo

designed to subconsciously prompt shopping
for laundry detergent. No, it is fire,
in even flares of bloom over dark boughs,

improbably reaching over the air and water station,
confident in its living florets of blood, spilled
extravagantly, for all. If you're looking,

you sense serene roots held in being,
lit by being. You catch the silent, steady burn
of the blossoms, the outpouring

of exuberant mercy. You want to remember
this always, this red apparition,
not for its existence, nor its flaming flowers,

but because it chooses as its companions
the empty tanks, the change-oil lights, the flat tires,
the ones who notice, and the ones who do not.

PINK MOMENT ON MULHOLLAND

The day had hammered with
abrupt losses—one expected, one tragic.

Our grief a sieve, we tried to make
soup, with everything short. Sent at dusk

for onion, ancho pepper, head bowed I
almost missed the sight,

everything suffused
sudden pink, the mountains blushing

tender, the roads all for home, buildings
linked reflecting pools of warmth,

the sky a glowing world, the world a rosy flush
if you were looking, only for this brief

moment, all open and extravagant
like a breath. Nothing could hold it.

Pepper fading already from our tongues,
dishes washed and put away, graying light

takes over, our words grapple and slip
through the fingers, off the page.

EVIDENCE OF A BURNING BUSH

Bed of blackened sugarbush bones lie,
a truth, now scorched claw struck down,

up in flames, obscure monument, a history,
a future. A burned bush, charred fallen hand,

a fist of silence, burning once for all and
none watched. Not burning bush untouched,

caressed by God in flame yet unconsumed,
ablaze on Horeb. These ebony fingers pointless,

purposefully indicate heavenward, soundless
shout, *I am evidence* and *I am beginning*,

an end accomplished, a sign for all to see, the
blind will not. Which, I wonder, is the stronger

weaker case for the groping heart in anguished
hope, the bush which burns bright without hurt

searing evermore, or the sugarbush that knows
unknown agony of inferno, brokenness, a death,

a life unsuspected in divine rejoinder, firedeath
birthing firelife, ashes for seed burst into being?

ABSENT WARNING

What if I told you the space between us
is the measure of one bird to the next,

the span of morning call
to answering chirp, wing rush to nest

in the maple, a glide to the apricot tree,
a hum rising above the bougainvillea.

Yet any home within a home is a glass orb
held softly on fingertips: a listless hand

drops dearness down for the shattering.
Have you seen the invisibility, the thinning

of the wings? The widening gaps, the mornings
quieter by thirty billion beaks? Wake up

to dawn without the chorus, melodies muted.
Open your eyes to blank boughs, badlands

swelling between us, how we vanish feathers
by the terrible power of our unseeing.

THE DEER

1.
I pass the oak, without seeing a lizard flick
down the trunk. I notice the not-legs
in the shadow on pavement, the horned
back arched, neck racing down, and I want
out of the shadow, into the blinding
care of light.

2.
I know the hurt within me as it is in you,
hidden in the dark twists and turns,
veins and nerves, matters burning
and dull, pressing.
You turn to slip out, to flee
the ache, then remember
you must climb.

3.
The path leads up the wall of mountain,
but do not look up, do not look down. Lock
on to the deer in the mid-distance,
the gentle dark eyes trained on you
cautiously, hooves tensed to you.
Will she sense peace or fear in you?
She knows them each, alternating
currents, sun and ice, grassland
and waste. Her life weighs in the morning
air like birdsong, short and supple. She bounds
with pump of heart, of breath; the chaparral
and poppies sway. This is the luster
of the shadow of your center,
the choice you make.

DRAWN
Ephesians 2:4–5

Even when we were dead you reached
us with your fiery fingers even deep in the dark

nether landscape, the flame at last catching, etching.
Not an easy thing to awaken to this burning, yet we turn

into the blistering luster of it, eager for the mistakes
to erase in smoke. Twice I have seen the walls of my home

glow orange. The first, an inferno of wildfire reflected
its destructive image there, an unnatural midnight sun flickering

over a drawing of you (a penciled desire of a drawing of you),
your eyes closed in prayer. The second, persimmons alight

in the dying autumn rays tinted the whole interior, a seeming
pastoral until I considered the still life of a body letting go

in bright-dappled yield. Both blazes revealed your consuming
mercy. Our wings home to it, our antennae prick

to the warm swelling updraft of it, the scoring and scorching
of the terrible approach, the blood-red falling away

of our transgressions. The likeness inside leaps to greet,
rushes to be brought to life, moths trembling into your

magnetic heat   as you render us in love.

TRANSMISSION

Red-tailed vortex of air   spiraling
above the freeway,   shimmering heat

of a thousand valley vehicles pulsing
a signal,   midday thermal currents invite

a dozen wheeling hawks.   A kettle
organizes   like a ladder of angels,

a summons   to float   freely,
immersed   in the higher   home.

My longing,   a grounded bird,
thrashes against the metal   and traffic but

they rest   on wings   of another
for a little, soar   on the flow, talons and

beaks   above and below,   on tongues
of exhaust.   They glory round

the cell tower, disguised as a too-emerald,
too-stiff palm.   They ring the blue finger

of God. The transmission   requires a path;
my displaced breath   of words the updraft,

a wrestling reach sunward,   carried high
and higher. The warmth,   the movement, the center

builds,   a wafting whole,   a transient channel,
permeable gyre   of connectivity,   a sky road even

wingless I could take: open the roof,   give my eyes
to the dazzle,   repeat like a mantra,   like Dorothy

in Oz,   like Mary of Bethany,   repeat
the need for only one thing.

TORCHLIGHT

Divine torches line
the way home.
Sugar maple
ruby fires
burn with delight.

Do they hide
inner suns?
They ignite
the very air
with scarlet glow.

In rushing joy
blazing hands stir,
caress coiling wind;
the dancing image
of living light.

In their ardor they
let go.
Crimson jewels fly,
become carpet,
vanish.

Naked branches yawn,
drowse in the gale,
dream of the hand that
kindles, stokes fire,
brings to life again.

PILLAR OF CLOUD, PILLAR OF FIRE

The thundercloud swirls, drape
of the divine brow
skids dark ahead of the howling

      wind, the one that drove cinders
      under my ready eaves

now slow splatters your drops
of mercy, casual as the rattle of dragonfly
wings skimming the surface of pond,

      flickering, translucent orange
      blaze of body so perfect, you

ripple the waters, crosshatch the laws
of physics, pour to overflowing
my cup. I open my mouth

      ashes to ashes, a mortal kiss
      for sparks of fire

and you fill it, flooding, fusing.
Let rain stream down my hair, my face
let it wash

      dust to dust, my particles
      your conflagration

me bright as the squirrel leaping up
wet branches, lithe furred sinew and bone
chasing. Draw me to our belonging.

      Inferno of a thousand suns,
      who can see you and live?

Let me, in this heartbeat, rise up
clear, alive
Let me, in this drenched moment

> in skin of you inflamed
> come forth as gold,

shimmer and shine of you.
Moses found you in the cloud
and his face

> burned incandescent with your love.

SUBSTANCE THEORY

The skin of the persimmon is not what it used to be

Who is to say that it is a less lovely sphere dulled to ripe auburn pulp
and although pecked, sun-patched.

The tree speaks them tenderly into being each season. Each in turn
turns to teach the turn to the one sweet heat.

A hachiya meets its appointments, matures beyond the astringent orange sheen,

reaching for Teresa reaching for Thérèse reaching for Teresa reaching
for the utter center of the divine diamond fruit, an arrow into flame

and in living flame, leaps and ignites the next. Incandescent
in the setting gold embrace, she gathers her ruddy round wisdom,

flares her warm fragrance on high:

I have kept both fresh and mellowed in store for you, my love.

I can say I love ardently, I will say we cradle stars.

I can say I hold the key, I will say we usher others through.

Root wither, wind bite and branch bend lead us here, a final kiss
for the crumbling leaf crown, a release of the heavy soft body

In the time of their visitation they will shine,
and dart about as sparks through stubble;

Perhaps you will just make out the glimmer of each autumnal halo in the dusk,
and it will light something inside, in the juiced middle, near the seed-heart

Who is to say the puckered rusted red flesh
is less lovely when it may be taken,
consumed, and dissolved
into molecules into
acid nebula into
fusion into
fire

ACKNOWLEDGMENTS

Grateful acknowledgment is made to the editors of the following publications in which some of these poems previously appeared, sometimes in a slightly different form:

ALTARWORK, "Over the Falls"

America: The Jesuit Review of Faith and Culture, "Substance Theory"

Anglican Theological Review, "Water-Walkers"

Carmelite Review, "St. John of the Cross Addresses the Dark Ray"

The Christian Century, "Organic Ink"

The Cresset, "The Eyes I Have Desired"

Cumberland River Review, "On the Efficacy of a Prophet"

Dappled Things, "The Eagle" and "Do you want to be well?"

Faith, Hope and Fiction, "Angel of Dark and Fire"

First Things, "Via Negativa: Mourning Dove"

In a Strange Land (Eugene, OR: Cascade Books, 2019) edited by D. S. Martin, "Good Fruit," "There is One Splendor of the Sun," and "Revelation"

NonBinary Review, "The Prince Decides"

The Penwood Review, "Pantoum of the Tinderbox"

Plum Tree Tavern, "Rain Comes in the Fourth Year"

Poems for Ephesians, "Drawn"

Poets Reading the News, "Absent Warning"

Relief: A Journal of Art and Faith, "Transmission"

Riddled with Arrows, "The Superfluous Hen"

Saint Katherine Review, "One Handful with Tranquility" and "The Tilling of Dorothy Day"

Santa Fe Literary Review, "Exodus"

Snapdragon: A Journal of Art & Healing, "The Breaking"

Solo Novo 7/8: Psalms of Cinder & Silt (Carpinteria, CA: Solo Press, 2019), "California Match Girl"

Whale Road Review, "Unexpected Wings"

The Windhover, "Nocturne," "Cherith," "Litany of Flights," and "Movable Feast"

"Nocturne," "Cherith," "Organic Ink," "Litany of Flights," and "The Eyes I Have Desired" also appeared in *In a Strange Land*, edited by D. S. Martin.

Sincere thanks also to Finishing Line Press for publishing several of these poems in the chapbook *O Garden-Dweller* (Georgetown, KY: Finishing Line Press, 2017).

I am deeply grateful to Jon M. Sweeney, Luci Shaw, and Mark S. Burrows for selecting this book as the winner of the 2020 Paraclete Poetry Prize.

Thank you to Elizabeth Kuelbs for her companionship in poetry, to Nan Cohen and Donna Spruijt-Metz for the close readings and loving support, and to Caitlin Hogan for her editorial intuition. Thank you to Sr. Ruth Burrows, OCD, for her friendship and responses to some of these poems.

I am grateful to all who have given me their kindness and generous support, especially Dana Gioia, Paul J. Willis, D. S. Martin, David Keplinger, Barbara Crooker, Katie Manning, Sofia Starnes, Robert Cording, Tania Runyan, Sally Thomas, Mischa Willett, A. M. Juster, Nathaniel Lee Hansen, Shannon Connor Winward, Leah Maines, Elline Lipkin, Blas Falconer, Phil Taggert, Marsha de la O, Glenna Luschei, Friday Gretchen, Mary Kay Rummel, Elaine Alarcon, Sr. Mary Clare Mancini, OCD, and Tim Bete. I thank the Napa Valley Writers' Conference, and Jane Hirshfield and Camille Dungy for their inspiration and wisdom. I am grateful to Paraclete Press, and in particular to Jon M. Sweeney, Publisher; Mark S. Burrows, Poetry Series Editor; Robert J. Edmonson, CJ, Managing Editor; and Rachel McKendree, Publicist.

To friends, my Lay Carmelite community, and my family, my abiding gratitude and love.

ABOUT PARACLETE PRESS

WHO WE ARE

As the publishing arm of the Community of Jesus, Paraclete Press presents a full expression of Christian belief and practice—from Catholic to Evangelical, from Protestant to Orthodox, reflecting the ecumenical charism of the Community and its dedication to sacred music, the fine arts, and the written word. We publish books, recordings, sheet music, and video/DVDs that nourish the vibrant life of the church and its people.

WHAT WE ARE DOING

BOOKS | PARACLETE PRESS BOOKS show the richness and depth of what it means to be Christian. While Benedictine spirituality is at the heart of who we are and all that we do, our books reflect the Christian experience across many cultures, time periods, and houses of worship.

We have many series, including *Paraclete Essentials*; *Paraclete Fiction*; *Paraclete Poetry*; *Paraclete Giants*; and for children and adults, *All God's Creatures*, books about animals and faith; and *San Damiano Books*, focusing on Franciscan spirituality. Others include *Voices from the Monastery* (men and women monastics writing about living a spiritual life today), *Active Prayer*, and new for young readers: *The Pope's Cat*. We also specialize in gift books for children on the occasions of Baptism and First Communion, as well as other important times in a child's life, and books that bring creativity and liveliness to any adult spiritual life. The MOUNT TABOR BOOKS series focuses on the arts and literature as well as liturgical worship and spirituality; it was created in conjunction with the Mount Tabor Ecumenical Centre for Art and Spirituality in Barga, Italy.

MUSIC | PARACLETE PRESS DISTRIBUTES RECORDINGS of the internationally acclaimed choir *Gloriæ Dei Cantores*, the *Gloriæ Dei Cantores Schola*, and the other instrumental artists of the *Arts Empowering Life Foundation*.

PARACLETE PRESS IS THE EXCLUSIVE NORTH AMERICAN DISTRIBUTOR for the Gregorian chant recordings from St. Peter's Abbey in Solesmes, France. Paraclete also carries all of the Solesmes chant publications for Mass and the Divine Office, as well as their academic research publications.

In addition, PARACLETE PRESS SHEET MUSIC publishes the work of today's finest composers of sacred choral music, annually reviewing over 1,000 works and releasing between 40 and 60 works for both choir and organ.

VIDEO | Our video/DVDs offer spiritual help, healing, and biblical guidance for a broad range of life issues including grief and loss, marriage, forgiveness, facing death, understanding suicide, bullying, addictions, Alzheimer's, and Christian formation.

Learn more about us at our website:
www.paracletepress.com
or phone us toll-free at 1.800.451.5006

SCAN TO READ

EXPLORE MORE OF PARACLETE POETRY...

EYE OF THE BEHOLDER
Luci Shaw

ISBN 978-1-64060-085-0 | Trade paperback | $18

"*Eye of the Beholder* awakens awareness of the extraordinary in the ordinary.... Shaw's poems are reminders of daily divinity: the wonders we might see if only we look closely enough, long enough."
—Nick Ripatrazone, *The Millions*

EXPLORING THIS TERRAIN
Margaret B. Ingraham

ISBN 978-1-64060-376-9 | Trade paperback | $19

"Braiding earnest religious longing into the memories and observations of an entirely earthly terrain, Ingraham's poems hold the lushness and ease of the rural South." —Taije Silverman

THE CONSEQUENCE OF MOONLIGHT
Sofia Starnes

ISBN 978-1-61261-860-9 | Trade paperback | $18

"With uncommon prosodic and linguistic elegance, Sofia Starnes brings to the onetime familiar an exhilarating vividness, a [re]vision that avails the story's ongoing opening, continuing agency." —Scott Cairns

Available at bookstores

Paraclete Press | 1-800-451-5006

www.paracletepress.com

www.ingramcontent.com/pod-product-compliance
Lightning Source LLC
Chambersburg PA
CBHW031124160426
43192CB00008B/1101